Florence
kid-sized

FIRENZE
MVSEI

texts: Barbara Conti
illustrations: Giulia Servello

ISBN 88-8347-280-2

A publication by
s i l l a b e s.r.l.
Livorno
www.sillabe.it
info@sillabe.it

managing editor: Maddalena Paola Winspeare
graphic design: Laura Belforte
editing: Giulia Bastianelli
translation: Emily Ligniti

Florence
kid-sized

8 itineraries for boys and girls through the city's streets

FIRENZE MVSEI

sillabe

A bit of history

The city was founded in 59 BC when the Romans built an encampment on the banks of the Arno River called *Florentia* in honor of the goddess Flora.

The center of the "new city" grew around a tall obelisk in what today is Piazza della Repubblica.

However, it was only towards the year 1000 that the city gained a certain level of importance, and in 1115 it formed a free Commune. It then tried to expand by waging war against nearby cities and imposing itself upon them.

Due to citizen disputes, in 1193 the city's government was entrusted to a *Podestà* (the name given to a high official) from another city. However, in 1250 Florence's merchants and artisans succeeded in having the government handed over to a *Capitano* (captain), chosen by them, and two councils made up of only the lower classes, in addition to the *Podestà*.

Over time, things settled down and in the early 14th century Florence was a rich and populous city. Despite the Black Death in 1348 and the economic and political crisis that followed, by the end of the century the city dominated most of Tuscany.

In 1434, Cosimo de' Medici had himself appointed Lord of Florence and his family began ruling the city. They were able to extend their control over all of Tuscany and receive the title of Grand Dukes.

In 1737, Gian Gastone died without an heir and so the Grand Duchy passed to the Lorraines, who introduced social and land reforms. They were exiled by the French in 1799 and Napoleon annexed Tuscany to his empire in 1807, entrusting it to his sister Elisa Baciocchi.

After the Congress of Vienna, the Lorraines returned to Florence, but in 1860 with the plebiscite Tuscany became part of the new Kingdom of Italy. Between 1865 and 1871, Florence was the capital. The urban works carried out during those years would later stifle her growth for a certain period of time.

In the early 20th century, Florence went through another positive phase: illustrious men of letters gave life to important magazines, new neighborhoods were formed, and numerous buildings were constructed. After the serious damage caused by World War II, Florence was once again hit hard by the flood of 1966. Today, after numerous ups and downs, tranquility and wellbeing have been restored.

Itinerary 1
the most important sites

From the Duomo to Palazzo Vecchio

Let me introduce myself: I'm **Arnolfo di Cambio**. Seeing I sculpted a few statues for the façade of the Duomo and I'm the architect of Palazzo Vecchio, I'll guide you along this itinerary.

via del proconsolo
via del corso
via dante alighieri
via de' cimatori
via della condotta
via de' cerchi
piazza della signoria
via dei tavolini
via degli speziali
via calimala
via porta rossa
via calimaruzza
via vacchereccia

This itinerary includes the city's most important religious buildings: the **Duomo** with the **Campanile** and the **Baptistery**.

The oldest monument in the square is precisely the **Baptistery**, dedicated to St. John, the protector of Florence. The outside is decorated with white and green marble, while on the inside the gold ceiling shines where a horrifying devil with horns, busy devouring sinners during Judgement Day, is depicted!

The Baptistery's three bronze doors are particularly precious, especially the one in front of the Duomo's façade: everyone calls it the *Porta del Paradiso* (Gates of Paradise) because it's so beautiful it deserves to be found there.

The original structure dates back to the 7th century, even though today its features are from the 11th–12th centuries.

The PORTA DEL PARADISO was made between 1425 and 1452 by Lorenzo Ghiberti, who represented a few scenes from the Old Testament on the door sections.

The **Duomo** (cathedral) is dedicated to Santa Maria del Fiore and it became famous in all the world especially for its dome in red bricks and white marble, which has become a symbol of Florence. It was quite a feat trying to build it, seeing that its base measures 52 meters!

Arnolfo di Cambio began building Santa Maria del Fiore in 1296: the work continued for years and was followed by many architects. The façade was made between 1871 and 1887.

The dome was built with revolutionary methods by Filippo Brunelleschi starting in 1420.

Giotto began work in 1334, but he died before it was finished. So, the work continued under the supervision of other architects until 1359.

Next to the cathedral you'll find the **Campanile** (bell tower) made by Giotto and covered in very elegant colored marble. 414 steps lead you to the roof with its panoramic terrace from which all of Florence can be seen.
Many large palaces face the square, including the Bishop's and those belonging to some of Florence's important families.

1

If you head down the centuries-old Via de' Calzaioli you'll reach **Piazza della Signoria**, or rather the social-political center of the city.

Begun at the end of the 13th century probably by Arnolfo di Cambio, it was the home of the Medici family, Lords of Florence, from 1540 to 1565. When the city was Italy's capital (1865–1871) it became the seat of the Chamber of Deputies. Today, it houses the Municipality's offices.

The square is undoubtedly one of the most beautiful in Florence and the Florentines have always tried to make it as representative as possible.
It's dominated by one of the most important medieval public palaces in Italy: **Palazzo Vecchio**, originally the seat of the *Priori*, who were responsible for governing the city. Today, the Town Hall is found here.
Over the course of the centuries,, it was rebuilt many times, both on the outside and the inside. In the first courtyard, you can admire the very lovely painted ceiling and the stucco decorations of the columns.

sculptures in the square

There are many sculptures on the sides of the square, but the **Neptune Fountain** stands out the most. It depicts the god of the sea, who is surrounded by sea divinities.
The statue, located to the left of the main entrance to Palazzo Vecchio, is especially famous. It represents the Biblical hero **David** who was able to defeat the giant Goliath by striking his head with a stone, thereby rescuing his people.
However, the original statue is in the Accademia Gallery. A copy was placed in the square (there's also another one in Piazzale Michelangelo, from where you can admire the most breathtaking view of the city).

DAVID, the original (p. 59) was sculpted by the great Michelangelo between 1501–1504.

NEPTUNE FOUNTAIN, made by Bartolomeo Ammannati who worked on it from 1563 to 1575.

Other heroes who triumphed over very powerful enemies are located nearby: to the right of the main entrance there's **Hercules** fighting the giant **Cacus**, who dared to steal some of his cattle but above all who terrorized with his fierceness the inhabitants of a part of the Latium region. By defeating him Hercules restored peace to that area.

A little over you'll see **Judith**, who cut off the head of the general **Holophernes**, thus saving her town. Very brave, she was able to enter the enemy camp and one evening, during a feast, she made Holophernes get drunk so she could kill him.

HERCULES AND CACUS, sculpted by Baccio Bandinelli in 1534.

JUDITH AND HOLOPHERNES, Donatello made this sculpture in around 1462.

sculptures in the square

In the square under the **Loggia dei Lanzi**, you'll see **Perseus**, the legendary Greek hero who with the help of the gods killed Medusa, a viscous creature who could turn men to stone with just one look.

Perseus cut off her head without staring at her directly in the eyes; he saw her reflection in a shiny shield given to him by the goddess Athena.

Another important group of sculptures under the Loggia is represented by the **Rape of the Sabine Women**. This is an

ancient Roman legend. Romulus, the first king of Rome, fortified and expanded the city, taking in just about all the "misfits" of the neighboring areas. Rome was above all populated by men and the inhabitants of the nearby cities refused to give their daughters in marriage to the Romans, who had the reputation of being rude and violent.

So Romulus ordered the abduction of the young Sabine women, who were dragged into the city against their will. The Sabines tried to free them by engaging in a bloody battle inside Rome. But their daughters were able to convince both sides to make peace.

PERSEUS, it's the most celebrated work of Benvenuto Cellini (1554).

RAPE OF THE SABINE WOMEN, this is one of Giambologna's most famous sculptures (1583).

Itinerary 2
a plunge into the Middle Ages

From Santa Croce to the Bargello

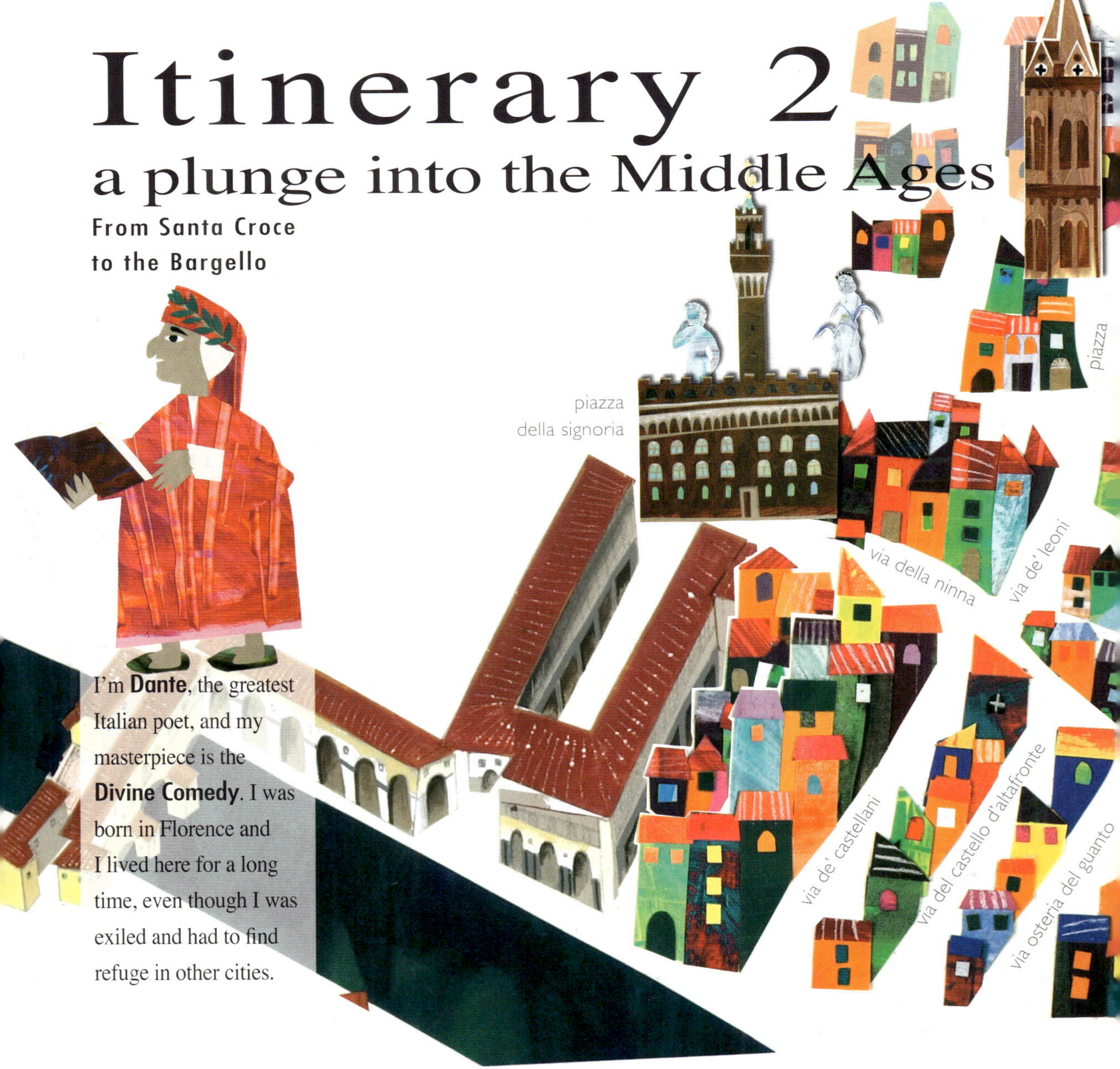

I'm **Dante**, the greatest Italian poet, and my masterpiece is the **Divine Comedy**. I was born in Florence and I lived here for a long time, even though I was exiled and had to find refuge in other cities.

isola delle stinche
via dei lavatoi
via ghibellina
via torta
via de' bentaccordi
via dell'anguillara
via verdi
via da verrazzano
via del fico
via de' pepi
via delle pinzochere
via san cristofano
borgo dei greci
piazza de' peruzzi
piazza santa croce
remigio
via de' benci
via delle brache
borgo santa croce
via dei neri

Piazza Santa Croce is dominated by the large Basilica built by Arnolfo di Cambio for the Franciscans.

2

It took about 90 years to build the Church (1295–1385). The façade was made in the second-half of the 19th century.

The reason why the square's so big is due to the friars: they initially used it for sermons, but later feasts and popular tournaments were held there as well.

In the Middle Ages, it became famous for horse jousting and the participants were awarded a scarf embroidered by a young Florentine woman.

Still today—during the festivities for St. John—the football matches of the **calcio storico fiorentino** are played in this square. This competition was, and still is, virile and harsh in nature: brawls, wrestling, and continuous hand-to-hand fighting for the ball toughened the spirit and toned the body of the citizens and especially of the legionaries who regularly participated.

Choosing the players (kickers) for the games was carefully done. The teams were made right in the square for the ordinary matches, but for the important games the players were selected in the palaces of the most important gentlemen in Florence.

Many eminent figures, from both the city and elsewhere, loved to try their hand at this game. Among the most noteworthy there were: Lorenzo de' Medici, Duke of Urbino; Alessandro de' Medici, Duke of Florence; Cosimo I, Grand Duke of Tuscany; Vincenzo Gonzaga, Duke of Mantua.

On the inside of the **Church of Santa Croce** there are numerous tombs of Italian artists, musicians, and writers from the past. Particularly evocative are a few chapels frescoed by Giotto with scenes from the lives of St. John and St. Francis.

The Capella Pazzi to the right of the Church is the work of the architect Filippo Brunelleschi, who began it in 1430 and supervised its construction until the year of his death, 1446.

As you head down Via Verdi, on the side of the square opposite the Church, and then Via Ghibellina, you'll reach the very old **Badia** and the **Palazzo del Bargello** with its tall tower (57 meters!).

The palace Courtyard: at the center you can see the well (where the legendary gallows was once found) and on the walls the coats-of-arms of the most prominent families in Florence.

Bargello: the palace was built at various times starting in 1255. Its tower was symbolically the tallest in the city; a law required all the others to be lowered.

The **Palazzo del Bargello** was the first residence of the Florentine government, when Palazzo Vecchio had not yet been built. Then it was turned into a prison ("Bargello" was the name of the justice *capitano*) and a few executions were carried out in the courtyard. But when Tuscany abolished the death penalty all the instruments used to kill the prisoners were burned right in the courtyard.
After various centuries, the palace became a museum. Today, it houses many sculptures, including a few works by Michelangelo, Donatello, Cellini, and Verrocchio.

the house-towers

The narrow streets found among Piazza della Signoria, the Duomo, the Bargello, and Piazza Santa Croce are the oldest in the city. In the Middle Ages, numerous fortified houses, the house-towers, a few of which can still be seen today, looked out onto these streets.

You can recognize them because they were built with long and narrow stones and rather small doors and windows so that the people inside could defend themselves from any attacks by their neighbors and prevent enemies from entering. In fact, during medieval times Florence was a cluster of small quarters that were continuously fighting with one another.

On the outside walls of the house-towers you can still see the holes that were once used to create temporary passages from one tower to the other with wooden planks.

Over the years, the ground floors were turned into workshops and gradually these house-towers became part of other constructions.

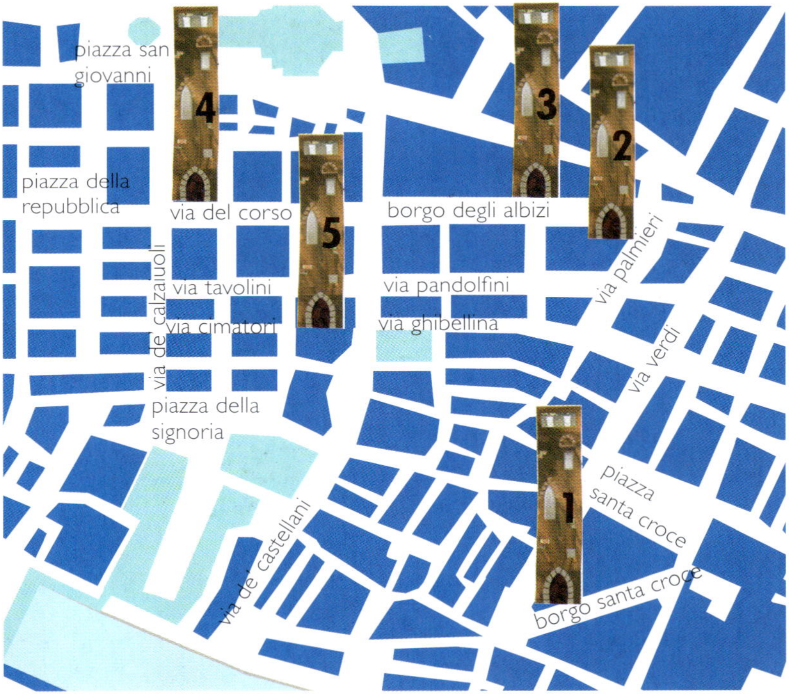

1. Borgo Santa Croce-corner Via de' Benci: Torre degli Alberti

2. Piazza San Pier Maggiore: Torre dei Donati, then Torre degli Albizzi

3. Borgo degli Albizzi-corner Piazzetta Calamandrei: Torre degli Albizzi

4. Via del Corso-corner Via Santa Elisabetta: Torre dei Donati, then Torre dei Ricci

5. Piazza San Martino: Torre della Castagna

largo f.lli alinari
via faenza
piazza madonna degli aldobrandini
piazza dell'unità d'italia
via panzani
via del giglio
via dell'alloro
via de' conti
via zannetti
borgo san lorenzo
piazza san lorenzo
via de' martelli
via de' banchi
via de' cerretani
via de' rondinelli
piazza antinori
via de' pecori
piazza san giovanni
via de' vecchietti
via brunelleschi
via de' tosinghi
via delle oche

Itinerary 3
the Medici Lords

**From Palazzo Medici-Riccardi
to San Lorenzo and the Medici Chapels**

In Florence, I designed the
Church of San Lorenzo, Santo Spirito,
and the Cappella dei Pazzi.
But my masterpiece is the Dome of
Santa Maria del Fiore, which I was able
to build without any armature:
am I or am I not a genius?
Oh, by the way, my name's
Filippo Brunelleschi.

3

The **Medici family**, wealthy Florentine bankers, had this impressive palace built and they lived here until 1540, which was when they moved into Palazzo della Signoria.

Palazzo Medici-Riccardi: built starting in 1444 by the architect Michelozzo for Cosimo the Elder de' Medici. It then passed on to the Riccardi family.

The *Three Magi on Horseback*: fresco by Benozzo Gozzoli (1459–1460). At the center, on a white horse, you'll see Lorenzo de' Medici.

Palazzo Medici-Riccardi became, ever since it was first built, a model for all the Florentines of the age. Seen from the outside, it is cube-shaped and divided into various strips: the lowest one is decorated with a *bugnato* motif, or rather with protruding stones (ashlar-work), and the other two strips seem lighter due to the many windows and the use of increasingly smoother stones. You can see the Medici coat-of-arms all around.
On the inside, there's a lovely courtyard and a frescoed chapel where the Medici commissioned a portrait of themselves dressed as the Three Magi.

3

The **Church of San Lorenzo** is tied to the Medici family, who financed its construction and celebrated all of the most important religious ceremonies there.

San Lorenzo: Filippo Brunelleschi worked on it starting in 1442; in the photo, you can see the complex in its entirety.

They called upon the most famous artists: Brunelleschi, the architect of the Duomo's Dome, was asked to design the basilica. Donatello was to decorate the **Sagrestia Vecchia** (old sacristy).

Later on, Michelangelo made the **Library** to house the Medici volumes and the **Sagrestia Nuova** (new sacristy) for the tombs of Lorenzo the Magnificent's son and grandson.

Then, Matteo Nigetti made the precious **Cappella dei Principi**, a chapel for the sarcophagi of the Grand Dukes of Tuscany, embellishing all of it with marble and semiprecious stones.

Today, the square around the church comes to life every day with the lively open-air market, and it's hard to see the monument to Giovanni dalle Bande Nere, a brave leader from the Medici family who died fighting against emperor Charles V.

Sagrestia Vecchia: designed by Brunelleschi and decorated by Donatello between 1435 and 1443.

Cappella dei Principi: the work of Matteo Nigetti, 17th century, based upon a drawing by Giovanni de' Medici, the family architect.

Sagrestia Nuova: begun by Michelangelo (1521–1524), it was later finished by Giorgio Vasari and Bartolomeo Ammannati.

Library: in 1524, Michelangelo planned the building and arranged the Library, designing the ceiling, book rests, and benches as well.

the unfinished façades

San Lorenzo and **Santa Maria del Carmine** have façades that are still incomplete: there's only the unfinished part with more or less protruding stones arranged in bands. These stones must have been used to support the slabs of marble that would cover the façade. Perhaps this can all be explained by the fact that the Florentines preferred to finish and adorn the inside before the outside. At times there were also unfavorable circumstances: with the façade of San Lorenzo, for example, Michelangelo was commissioned to elaborate a project, but the two heirs of the Medici family who had hired the artist unexpectedly died. As a result, Michelangelo had to move on to the Sagrestia Nuova. And so, despite his effort, the façade was never completed.

Miniature model of the façade of San Lorenzo: this is the wooden model based on a drawing by Michelangelo found in the Museum of Casa Buonarroti.

The façade of San Lorenzo and of Santa Maria del Carmine: the color is due to the uncut stones that were supposed to be covered with slabs of marble.

John B. Philpot, The church of Santa Croce in Florence in a photograph, ca 1857: compare it to the present-day façade on page 18.

Itinerary 4
strolling through the Oltrarno

From Santo Spirito to Santa Maria del Carmine

I'm **Masaccio**, one of the most important Florentine painters from the 15th century. I'm able to depict real space, volume, and light, as has never been done before. In a nutshell, you could say I'm revolutionary!

ponte alla carraia
piazza
nazario sauro
via de' serragli
via maffia
via santo
spirito
lungarno guicciardini
ponte santa trinita
piazza
santo spirito
via sant'agostino
via maggio
via de' vellutini
via de' guicciardini
borgo tegolaio
via mazzetta
via delle caldaie
piazza
san felice
piazza de' pitti

Piazza Santo Spirito was a big clearing that, as with the others in the city, was used to host performances, feasts, and sermons. It was later transformed, and the large central fountain and the centuries-old trees give the square a rather particular look.

Piazza Santo Spirito: during the first-half of the 19th century the architect Giuseppe del Rosso moved the fountain from the first convent cloister to the middle of the square, which he later embellished with trees and bushes.

In the background, you'll see the simple plaster façade of one of the most beautiful churches in Florence, **Santo Spirito**, and the work of Filippo Brunelleschi. The money needed to build the church was collected from among the inhabitants of the neighborhood, and one of the most well-to-do inhabitants guaranteed to personally add more money in case the sum wasn't enough.

However, the work was interrupted when Brunelleschi died, then was resumed by his students, but a fire destroyed a part of the church, thereby delaying work even more. It took 44 years to complete, not including the bell tower!

To the left of the church there's the Augustinian Convent that, thanks to its noteworthy collection of rare books, has become an important center of culture. Numerous scholars have come here.

Church of Santo Spirito: begun by Brunelleschi in 1444 but finished only in 1488. The bell tower was built in 1503 by Baccio d'Agnolo.

4

If you go down Via Sant'Agostino and then Via Santa Monaca, you'll arrive in **Piazza del Carmine** where you'll find the **Church of Santa Maria del Carmine**, famous especially for its frescoes by Masolino and Masaccio in the **Cappella Brancacci**.

In fact, it was customary to fresco the inside of churches, and every important family had its own private chapel, for which it commissioned paintings and ornaments.

The frescoes in the **Cappella Brancacci** depict scenes from the Bible, the Gospels, and the life of St. Peter. Fortunately, they were spared from a fire that destroyed a large section of the church, which was later rebuilt almost entirely.

The **square** on the outside is irregular in shape because it was created by demolishing another church and uniting two different squares. In the past, sacred performances for the feast of the Ascension were held here with the participation of the most important artists that created spectacular scenographies.

Santa Maria del Carmine: medieval in origin, it was later rebuilt after the fire of 1771 and finished in 1775.

Cappella Brancacci: *Tribute Money* by Masaccio, below *Resurrection of the Son of Theophilus* and *St. Peter on his Throne*, by Masaccio and Filippino Lippi. The frescoes were begun in 1424 and completed in 1480.

Florentine tabernacles

Tabernacles are sacred images located at the corners of streets and intended for popular devotion. In Florence, there are about 1,200 of them, and a few were made by important artists.
In front of many of these, masses were oftentimes held and—once prayers were over—small oil lamps were lit so as to bear witness to the faith of the inhabitants even at night. Moreover, they also helped to light the streets.
During periods of plague—like, for example, the Black Death in 1348—people avoided going to church for fear of being infected. So the tabernacles were the only place where the faithful could pray. In the neighborhoods of the Oltrarno, there are still a few left right in the vicinity of Piazza Santo Spirito and Piazza del Carmine.

1. Piazza Santo Spirito corner Via delle Caldaie: *Madonna*
2. Via Santa Monaca corner Via de' Serragli: Bicci di Lorenzo, *Madonna and Child between Saints Paul and Jerome*, 1427. At the feet of the Madonna the commissioner is depicted on his knees.
3. Via del Leone corner Via della Chiesa: Giottino, *Madonna and Child with Angels and Saints*, late 14th century. Originally it was located in Piazza Santo Spirito, but was moved in the 18th century. The image—called the "Madonna del Morbo" (Madonna of the Plague)—was perhaps made as a sign of thanks that the 1348 epidemic had finished. Today it has been replaced with a copy made by L. Benini in 1958.
4. Piazza del Carmine corner Piazza Piattellina: Pietro Gerini, *Madonna and Saints.*
5. Piazza del Carmine corner Borgo San Frediano: *Sacred Family.*
6. Piazza del Carmine corner Via Santa Monaca: Alessio Baldovinetti, *Madonna and Child with St. John* and the commissioner on his knees.

FIUME ARNO
borgo san frediano
via del leone
piazza del carmine
via della chiesa
via de' serragli
piazza santo spirito
1
2
3
4
5
6

piazza dell'unità
d'italia
piazza madonna
degli aldobrandini
via de' conti
via della scala
via panzani
via degli avelli
via dell'alloro
via palazzuolo
piazza
santa maria novella
via de' banchi
piazza san paolino
via de' rondinelli
via della porcellana
via del sole
piazza degli
ottaviani
via de' pescioni
via de' vecchietti
via della spada
lungarno amerigo vespucci
via de' fossi
piazza de'
rucellai
via della vigna nuova
via de' federighi
via purgatorio
via tornabuoni
via del parione
lungarno corsini
via porta rossa
ponte alla carraia

Itinerary 5

an illustrious neighborhood

From Santa Maria Novella to Palazzo Rucellai, Palazzo Strozzi, and Santa Trinita

I worked for many years in the city, building palaces and churches and finishing the façade of Santa Maria Novella. But I also traveled a lot and built things in many other Italian cities. My name is **Leon Battista Alberti.**

Piazza Santa Maria Novella is another important place in Florence. It's closed off on one side by the Church and by the Dominican convent, and on the other side by the loggia of the ancient Hospital of San Paolo, adorned with terracotta medallions by Luca and Andrea della Robbia.

Giovanni Signorini, *Palio dei Cocchi in Piazza Santa Maria Novella*, 1844. Florence, Pitti Palace, Gallery of Modern Art.

In the square you can see the obelisks that were originally made from wood and which today rest upon bronze turtles made by Giambologna.

The square looks different today than it did in the past, when the flowerbeds and central fountain weren't present. The square was completely empty so that the **Palio dei Cocchi** could take place. This was a competition that called to mind ancient Roman ones, with chariots drawn by pairs of horses that had to race around the square a few times, turning round the obelisks that can still be seen today.

The **Church of Santa Maria Novella** (once called "delle Vigne" for its rural surroundings) has always been the boundary for the most external part of the city. However, seeing that for a certain period of time the façade was incomplete, a wealthy Florentine volunteered to finance the work needed to finish it. He entrusted the architect Leon Battista Alberti to come up with a solution. The result is particularly harmonious, especially thanks to the two very elegant volutes, all inlaid with marble, which serve to hide the slanting of the roof. There are many masterpieces inside the church: frescoes by Masaccio and Ghirlandaio, the marvelous crucifixes by Giotto and Brunelleschi.

Santa Maria Novella: it was built by Dominican architects—Fra Sisto da Firenze and Fra Ristoro da Campi—beginning in 1278. It was completed towards the mid-14th century. The façade was designed by Leon Battista Alberti, who made the main portal and frieze (1458–1470). The inside is divided into three wide naves, and here you can see the central one.

If you take Via de' Fossi and then make a left onto Via della Vigna Nuova until Via Tornabuoni, you'll come across a few of the most beautiful **Renaissance palaces** in the city.

Palazzo Rucellai: was built in the mid-15th century by Bernardo Rossellino and based upon the project of Leon Battista Alberti.

Palazzo Strozzi: was begun in 1489 by Benedetto da Maiano and continued by Cronaca, who was also responsible for the impressive inside courtyard. The work continued at various times until 1538.

Church of Santa Trinita: it dates back to the 12th century, but was rebuilt in the 14th century. The façade is the work of Bernardo Buontalenti.

On Via della Vigna Vecchia you'll find the palace built for Giovanni **Rucellai**, the wool merchant who sponsored the façade of Santa Maria Novella. It was planned by Leon Battista Alberti, conceiving for Rucellai a new architectonic layout that is very light and elegant.
The stone bench on the street—which was once also used to mount horses—will make you want to linger in the small square, closed off by the loggia, which the family used for feasts and ceremonies.

Once you've arrived on Via Tornabuoni you'll see the back of the palace built for the very wealthy **Strozzi** family, which was based upon the most important ones already present in the city. This impressive palace is also a symbol of the power the family achieved.

Continuing along the same street heading towards the Arno you'll come to the **Church of Santa Trinita** with its austere stone façade. Here, the Strozzi family had their own chapel and a few tombs. Actually, the square is an intersection of streets, surrounded by lovely palaces.

A few columns in the squares of Florence's center commemorate important events of the city's past.

The one in Piazza Santa Trinita was erected in the place where Cosimo I received the news that the rebel republican army had been defeated. It is topped by a statue depicting Justice. Its "twin" in Piazza San Felice is also tied to this event.

The Croce al Trebbio ("trebbio" comes from the Latin "trivium," or where three roads meet) gave its name to the small square, in which bloody religious battles were fought.

In Piazza San Giovanni, next to the Baptistery, you'll find a column decorated with a bronze tree in the place where an elm turned green again when it came into contact with the coffin of St. Zanobi, brought from the church of San Lorenzo in order to be buried in the cathedral. Instead, the one in Piazza della Repubblica, with the statue of Abundance marks the center of the ancient Roman forum. And finally, the column in Piazza Santa Felicita was rebuilt after the bombings of World War II and originally it held up the statue of St. Peter Martyr.

1. Piazza Santa Felicita, column with St. Peter Martyr
2. Piazza della Repubblica, column of Abundance
3. Piazza Santa Trinita, column of Justice
4. Piazza San Felice, column of St. Peter Martyr
5. Piazza San Giovanni, small column of St. Zanobi
6. Piazza della Croce al Trebbio, column of the Croce al Trebbio

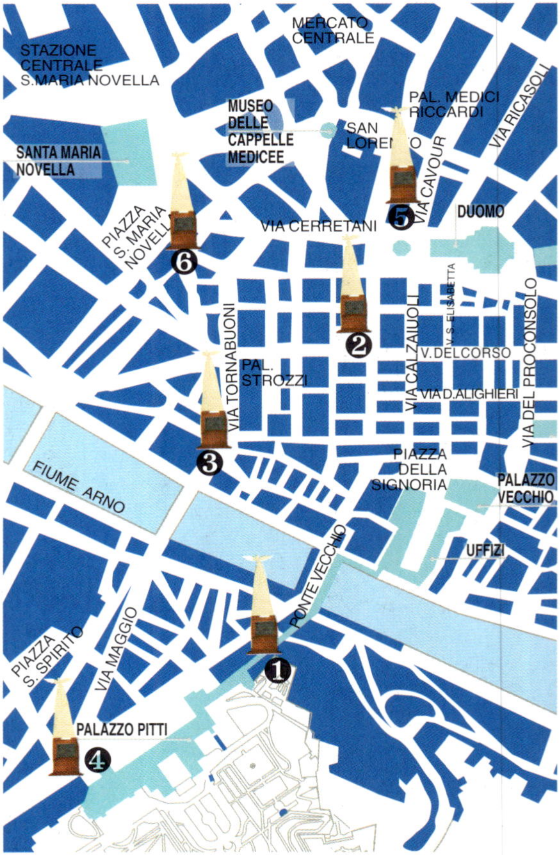

Piazza della Repubblica: statue of Abundance

Piazza Santa Trinita: column of Justice

Itinerary 6
the palaces of the Grand Dukes

From the Uffizi to Pitti Palace and the Boboli Gardens

I'm **Eleonora da Toledo**, daughter of the Viceroy of Naples and wife of Cosimo I de' Medici. For our big family I bought Pitti Palace at the cost of 9,000 gold florins. I had it enlarged, calling upon famous architects and artists to decorate it.

lungarno guicciardini
ponte santa trinita
lungarno acciaiuoli
por santa maria
via de' baroncelli
piazzale degli uffizi
via maffia
piazza
santo spirito
via del presto di san martino
via maggio
via dello sprone
via de' guicciardini
lungarno de' medici
costa san giorgio
via mazzetta
borgo tegolaio
via de' bardi
via del canneto
piazza
san felice
costa
scarpuccia
piazza de' pitti

6

Piazza della Signoria extends towards the Arno and the **Uffizi** courtyard, which is surrounded by loggias. Cosimo I de' Medici wanted the Uffizi to be built so that he could have the offices of the Grand Duchy there. In fact, the word "uffizi" means offices.

Uffizi: built by Giorgio Vasari between 1560–1580; the statues were placed there between 1842 and 1856.

In order to make room for his project, the Grand Duke didn't hesitate to expropriate the houses in this centuries-old neighborhood and then de-

molish them. The painter and architect Giorgio Vasari was commissioned. Despite the limited amount of space available, Vasari was able to create a building that wasn't too overwhelming. It's U-shaped and therefore not closed off on all four sides; in fact, one side of the courtyard opens up onto the Arno.

Under the loggia you can still see the inlaid wooden doors of the offices with different markings or symbols that distinguished one from the other.

The 28 statues in the niches were made only many years later: the project was intended to celebrate the most illustrious Tuscans by having their portraits sculpted by artists from the region. Public lotteries were held in which numerous citizens took part to finance the idea.

Today, the **Uffizi Gallery** is located in the building. The Gallery is one of the most beautiful and important museums in the world. It houses some of the greatest masterpieces of art, most of which come from the private collections of the Medici family.

Sandro Botticelli, *The Birth of Venus*, ca 1484: the painting was once found in the villa Cosimo I owned at Castello, near Florence.

Bernardo Buontalenti, Tribuna, 1584: this marvellous room contained the most valuable treasures of the Medici collection.

6

After reaching Ponte Vecchio and then continuing along Via Guicciardini, you'll reach **Piazza Pitti** with its grandiose palace.

The Pitti family wanted a residence that would show everyone how rich they were and be the biggest in the city. They spent a fortune to build what today is the central part of the palace (the side extensions and the two wings that close off the sides of the square were added later on).

In 1549, the Medici family bought it with the dowry of Eleonora da Toledo, wife of Cosimo I, so they could live in a house

Pitti Palace: built by Luca Fancelli, student of Brunelleschi, and probably based upon the teacher's drawing in around 1458. The Medici family moved here in 1550. It was enlarged by Bartolomeo Ammannati and Giulio Parigi starting in 1558. It took its present-day shape, with the two wings that come forth on the sides of the square, at the end of the 18th century.

Buontalenti Grotto, 1583-1593: the inside is decorated with frescoes and statues of wild animals.

Amphitheater, 17th century: open-air performances were held here, and it's embellished with an obelisk from Luxor and pottery from the Baths of Caracalla in Rome.

that was suited to their social rank as Grand Dukes. They embellished it in an even more spectacular way, creating the courtyard where performances and plays of naval battles were held. They were also responsible for creating the Boboli Gardens (an unbelievable 45,000 square meters!) that extends up the hill until Forte Belvedere.

This was the residence of all the Grand Dukes—first the Medicis and later the Hapsburg-Lorraines. Then for a short time it was the home of the King of Italy, Vittorio Emanuele II.

Today, 7 important museums are found here: the Palatine Gallery, which houses the paintings of the Medici family; the Gallery of Modern Art; the "Medici Treasury"; the Carriage Gallery; the Porcelain Museum; the Costume Gallery; the Boboli Gardens.

Raphael, *Madonna and Child with St. John ("Madonna della seggiola")*, ca 1516.

the bridges over the river

Florence's bridges have all collapsed and been rebuilt through the years—for the last flooding of the Arno in 1966 or for the German bombings during World War II. During those years, only Ponte Vecchio wasn't destroyed, though it was mined at both ends but not completely eliminated like the others.

The first to be built during Roman times was **Ponte Vecchio** that, over the centuries, was filled with artisan workshops. Initially, there were the more popular ones, like the butcher and shoemaker shops. But then Grand Duke Ferdinando I wanted only goldsmith shops so that the view from the Vasari Corridor, which passes right above the bridge and was often used by him to get from the Uffizi to Pitti Palace without being seen, would be more pleasant.

Heading up the Arno on the other side of Ponte Vecchio you can admire **Ponte alle Grazie**, which resisted the flooding of the river on various occasions. As a sign of thanks, the Florentines erected

tabernacles and small oratories and, before it was bombed, this bridge looked something like Ponte Vecchio.

Downstream there's **Ponte Santa Trinita**. The original was in wood and was rebuilt three times before Grand Duke Cosimo I entrusted the work to the court architect, Bartolomeo Ammannati. The great Michelangelo was also consulted various times and in the end an elegant and scenographic bridge was created, adorned at the ends by statues representing the seasons. The bridge we see today was rebuilt after 1944 but it is exactly the same in shape as the original one.

Further down the river there's **Ponte alla Carraia**, the second (in chronological order) built over the Arno. The original was knocked down when the river flooded, and once it was put back together again it collapsed due to the weight of spectators during a performance. Ammannati rebuilt it once again, but it lasted until World War II.

Itinerary 7
convents and precious museums

From the Accademia to Santissima Annunziata and the Archaeological Museum

I'm **Michelangelo**, the artist who sculpted the *David*, famous in all the world. In Florence, I worked for the Medici family as an architect and sculptor, and my works are kept in many of the city's museums. But I was often called to Rome by the Pope and I left great masterpieces there as well.

via santa reparata
via san gallo
via la pira
via micheli
piazza san marco
via alfani
via battisti
piazza
santissima
annunziata
via ricasoli
via de' servi
via della colonna

Piazza San Marco is a space enclosed between a church and other buildings, including the Accademia di Belle Arti and its portico decorated with terracotta lunettes.

7

The façade of the Church is rather elegant; it's in stone with marble statues and has above a large bas-relief depicting St. Antonino, Bishop of Florence and prior of the convent of San Marco, as he blesses the city.

To the right of the church you'll see the museum, located on the inside of the Dominican convent. Cosimo the Elder came to this convent on spiritual retreats, and he had a library built here. You can still visit the cells of the friars frescoed by **Beato Angelico**, who lived here.

The Cloister of St. Antonino: created during the initial phases of renovation work by Michelozzo (1437–1440), in the same years in which Beato Angelico was decorating the complex.

This *Annunciation*, ca 1440, is one of the few frescoes Beato Angelico painted outside the cells.

Next to the Accademia, in Via Ricasoli, there's the museum that houses the most famous sculptures by Michelangelo: the ***David***, the *Slaves*, and *St. Matthew*.
The *David* was brought here from Piazza Signoria by using a large cart built by a train engineer that moved along tracks on the street. It took 7 days and finally the large sculpture entered the room built to house it—known as the Tribuna—before the walls were raised around it.

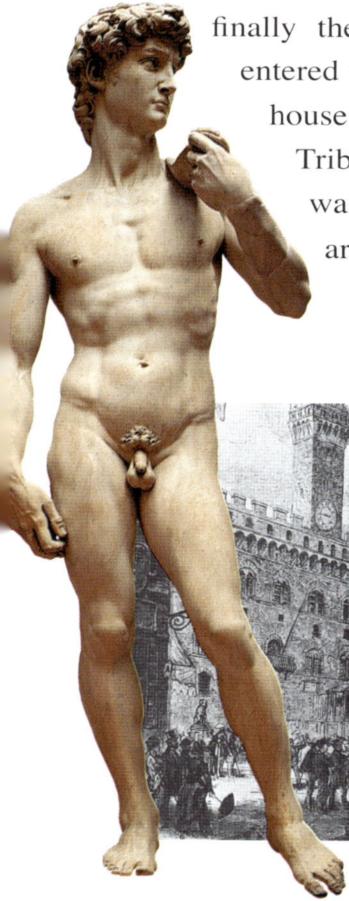

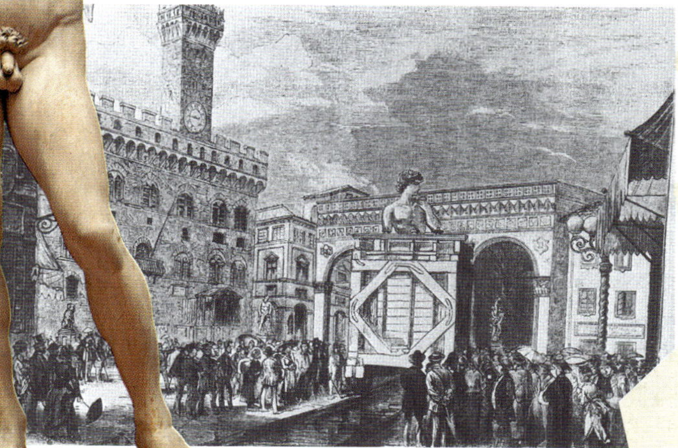

Slaves: made by Michelangelo in 1530 for the tomb of Pope Julius II.

David: made by Michelangelo in 1501–1504; it was placed in the Accademia Gallery in 1872.
Moving the *David* from Piazza della Signoria to the Accademia Gallery, from *Nuova Illustrazione Universale*, 1874.

7

Walking down Via Cesare Battisti you'll arrive in **Piazza Santissima Annunziata**, surrounded by porticoes.

Besides the one belonging to the **Church of the Annunziata**, there's the loggia of the Ospedale degli Innocenti, an orphanage, decorated with sky-blue majolicas, and the one with the coat-of-arms of the Servi di Maria, who were responsible for having the Church built.
Pilgrims took shelter here. For the September 8 feast-day they would arrive during the night from the countryside and lay down here to rest as they waited for the doors of the sanctuary, dedicated to the Madonna, to open.
Today, on this same September day, the feast of the *rificolona*, the paper lantern with which the peasants would light up the street, is celebrated in this square.

The Loggiato dei Serviti: by Antonio da San Gallo il Vecchio and Baccio d'Agnolo, 1516–1525.

Right near the square, on Via della Colonna, you'll see the entrance to the **Archaeological Museum**, which houses important archaeological finds from Egyptian and Etruscan civilizations, including the *Chimera* found in Arezzo.

The Palazzo della Crocetta, built in 1619–1620 by Giulio Parigi. It has housed since 1881 the National Archaeological Museum.

Chimera, late 5th–early 4th BC: it is a monstrous animal with two heads, one of a lion and one of a goat, with a snake's tail

Church of the Annunziata: it dates back to 1250, but the way it looks today is from 1444–1477 and was made by Michelozzo and, later, Leon Battista Alberti.

The Loggiato degli Innocenti: by Filippo Brunelleschi, 1419, with majolicas by Andrea della Robbia.

fountains and horses

Both in Piazza della Signoria and in Santissima Annunziata you'll see Grand Dukes Cosimo I and Ferdinando I represented on horseback as great leaders. Both statues were commissioned by Ferdinando, who perhaps was inspired by ancient Roman ones. They were modeled by the court sculptor Giambologna, who at the base of the one found in Piazza Santissima Annunziata placed the emblem of Ferdinando—a beehive with the queen bee at the center.

Particularly original are the bronze fountains of the Annunziata. They were commissioned by Ferdinando I to Pietro Tacca—the student and successor of Giambologna as court sculptor—for the port of Livorno. This is why a marine motif consisting in intertwined shells and mollusks was chosen as the decoration. Cosimo II betrayed his father's intention and placed the fountains in Piazza Santissima Annunziata.

Giambologna and Pietro Tacca, *Equestrian Statue of Ferdinando I*, 1608

Pietro Tacca, *Fountain with sea monsters*, 1629

costa scarpuccia
lungarno torrigiani
piazza demidoff
costa san giorgio
via dei renai
viale
via di belvedere
via dell'erta canina
via di san leonardo
passo all'erta
viale galileo galilei
piazza ungarelli

Itinerary 8
the city seen from above

From Forte Belvedere to San Miniato and Piazzale Michelangelo

My name, **Giuseppe Poggi**, is remembered because I planned the streets in Florence when the city became the capital of the Kingdom of Italy from 1865 to 1871. The large terrace of Piazzale Michelangelo, from which you'll have a marvelous view of Florence, is one of my creations.

8

Beginning in Roman times, Florence was surrounded by **walls** so that it could defend itself from possible outside attacks. As the number of inhabitants grew and the city got bigger and bigger, the walls were modified and enlarged.

Forte Belvedere was part of the city's defensive system, but the Grand Dukes really wanted it so that they could protect themselves from citizen uprisings instead of outside threats. Its cannons were aimed at numerous places in Florence, even though they were never used.
The fort borders on the Boboli Gardens, which connect it to Pitti Palace. By crossing the Garden, the Grand Dukes could quickly take shelter in the fort without having to walk in the street. As a refuge for the Medici family, the small palace found at the center was built. The fort was opened to the public in the second-half of the 20th century, and today art exhibitions are held here.

Forte Belvedere: wanted by Ferdinando I—son of Cosimo I—and built by Bernardo Buontalenti and Giovanni de' Medici between 1590 and 1595.

8

If you walk down the evocative Via San Leonardo, you'll reach Viale Galileo and from there the **Basilica of San Miniato al Monte**, decorated with geometric designs in white and green marble.

It's dedicated to the first Florentine Christian martyr, who is depicted in the façade mosaic to the right of Christ as he takes off his crown and exchanges it for a halo. In front of the church, the square isn't big because the steep hill upon which it was built cannot allow for anything bigger, but it's a charming panoramic point.

Basilica of San Miniato: the Church is a masterpiece of Florentine Romanesque architecture; it was built between 1018 and 1207 with small arches and geometric decorations that stand out because of the colored marble.

Piazzale Michelangelo is also famous for its view: it's adorned with a bronze sculpture group that reproduces a few works of the master artist Michelangelo. The loggias on the opposite side of the long window-lined balcony were intended to be used as a museum dedicated to Michelangelo, but the project was never realized and today the building has become a restaurant.

Piazzale Michelangelo: was made in around 1875 precisely to enjoy a wonderful view of the city.

The technique for building the walls around Florence involved, in the first place, creating gates along the entrances to the city, with solid wooden doors reinforced with iron nails so as to stop any wrongdoers from entering.

Towers were erected above the gates that allowed guards to keep watch over the entrances. These were then joined with moats and stockades and finally with embattled walls.

Initially, the entire circle of walls had a communication trench for the patrols. Recently, a short stretch behind Porta Romana has been reopened and can be reached from the square by walking down Viale Galileo and Viale Machiavelli. By entering from Viale Petrarca and going up a few steps you'll reach the top of the walls above the ancient south entrance to the city, which was guarded from above through iron bars and openings.

Today, only few sections of the walls remain, seeing that the greatest part was demolished during the 19th century in order to make room for wide avenues. Instead, the gates have remained intact and can be seen in the center of squares created just for them.

Francesco di Lorenzo Rosselli, *Perspective view called "della Catena"* (19th-century copy). Museum Firenze com'era. The city is represented from a bird's-eye view and is surrounded by walls with tall towers and gates.

Porta Romana: dates back to 1328–1331 and it's the only one that still has its original doors.

printed in September 2005
by Genesi, Città di Castello
for sillabe